Delta Force
in Action

SPECIAL OPS

by Gail Blasser Riley

Consultant: Fred Pushies
U.S. SOF Adviser

BEARPORT
PUBLISHING

New York, New York

Credits

Cover and Title Page, © MC2 Eli J. Medellin; 4, © Les Stone/ZUMA Press/newscom.com; 5, © Steve Starr/CORBIS; 6, © AP Images; 7, © Bettmann/CORBIS; 8, © Chris Hondros/Getty Images; 9, © Erik S. Lesser/Getty Images; 10, © Technical Sergeant H.H. Deffner; 11, © REUTERS/Tami Chappell; 12, © Joe Stewartson/MCT/newscom.com; 13, © TSGT Rob Marshall; 14, © Stephen Jaffe/AFP/Getty Images; 15, © Michael Lemke; 16, © U.S. Army photo by Martin Greeson; 17, © CORBIS; 18, © A1C Martin Limon; 19, © U.S. Air Force photo by Staff Sgt. DeNoris A. Mickle; 20, © Attar Maher/CORBIS SYGMA; 21, © AP Images/Raouf; 22, © AP Images/Mark Duncan; 23, © AP Images/Kathy Willens; 24, © Tyler Hicks/The New York Times/Redux; 25, © Cheryl Diaz Meyer/Dallas Morning News/Corbis; 26, © Leif Skoogfors/CORBIS; 27, © PHAN Pedro A. Rodriguez, USN; 28T, © Fred Pushies; 28B, © Boeing photo/Ron Bookout; 29T, © Fred Pushies; 29M, © REUTERS/Philippines; 29B, © John Yoder.

Publisher: Kenn Goin
Senior Editor: Lisa Wiseman
Creative Director: Spencer Brinker
Design: Debrah Kaiser
Photo Researcher: Amy Dunleavy

Note: Due to the highly secret nature of their work, there are no photos of **current** Delta Force operators in this book.

Library of Congress Cataloging-in-Publication Data

Riley, Gail Blasser.
  Delta Force in action / by Gail Blasser Riley.
      p. cm. (Special ops)
  Includes bibliographical references and index.
  ISBN-13: 978-1-59716-635-5 (library binding)
  ISBN-10: 1-59716-635-9 (library binding)
  1. United States. Army. Delta Force—History—Juvenile literature. I. Title.

UA34.S64R55 2007
356'.167—dc22
                                                  2007042063

For more information, write to Bearport Publishing Company, Inc., 101 Fifth Avenue, Suite 6R, New York, New York 10003. Printed in the United States of America in North Mankato, Minnesota.

022011
021011CGC

10 9 8 7 6 5

Contents

Enemy Prison Rescue

In an instant, the lights went out! The entire **prison** was pitch-black. American **hostage** Kurt Muse heard gunfire outside his cell. He had been a prisoner in Panama for many months. Would he soon be rescued?

An American soldier in Panama in 1989

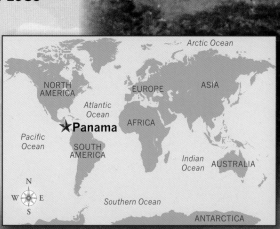

Four **choppers** carrying Delta Force **operators** touched down on the prison roof. The soldiers raced toward the prison entrance and blew down the door with **explosives**. They ran inside, fighting the enemy as they forced their way through the smoke-filled building. Bullets zipped by. Finally, Delta Force operators found Muse's cell. They blasted open the door and took Muse to the helicopters on the roof.

American soldiers prepare for a mission in Panama in 1989.

Kurt Muse had been **kidnapped** because he was trying to help put an end to Panama's dangerous government. He was rescued by Delta Force in 1989.

The Need for Delta

The brave soldiers who rescued Kurt Muse were part of a special group called Delta Force. This group began more than 30 years ago. Why was it formed? During the early 1970s, **terrorism** was growing quickly throughout the world. Terrorists often attacked and kidnapped Americans in other countries.

U.S. soldiers in the early 1970s

Army Colonel Charles Beckwith believed the United States needed a special army group to fight terrorism. He worked hard to convince others in the U.S. Army to agree with his ideas. In 1977, he succeeded. Delta Force was formed.

Army Colonel Charles Beckwith

Much of Delta Force's work is kept secret. This is necessary to allow Delta Force operators to surprise the enemy.

The Beginning of Delta Force

Colonel Beckwith was put in charge of organizing Delta. He had to decide who would serve as Delta operators.

Delta Force training began at Fort Bragg in North Carolina.

Beckwith knew that Delta operators would fight the most dangerous enemies. He realized they would handle some of the hardest **missions** in the world. He looked for soldiers who were strong, smart, and fearless. Beckwith needed the best soldiers in the U.S. Army.

To try out for the first Delta Force **unit**, a soldier had to be at least 22 years old, pass a swim test while wearing heavy boots and a uniform, pass the Rangers/Special Forces **physical** training test, and pass a written test.

The Very Best

One of the soldiers Beckwith considered for the first Delta Force unit was Eric Haney. Haney was an **Army Ranger**. He served as a **jumpmaster**. This was one of the toughtest jobs in the army. He made sure all the **parachute jumpers** on a plane jumped safely. He had all the right skills to become a Delta Force operator.

A jumpmaster (right) gives a soldier commands before a jump.

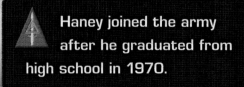

Haney joined the army after he graduated from high school in 1970.

One day in 1977, Haney was leading a jump. Along with other army soldiers, he zipped through the air in a plane going 120 miles per hour (193 kph). When it was time for the jump, Haney gave the command. Each soldier leaped out of the plane. Then, Haney made his own jump and landed safely on the ground.

Army Rangers parachuting out of a plane at Fort Benning in Georgia

Making the Cut

Haney soon learned that he had been invited to try out for a new army group—Delta Force. He had been selected because he was smart, fast, and brave. Haney knew that the missions of the Delta Force would be dangerous and hard. He also knew his work would have to be kept completely secret.

Eric Haney is one of the **founding** operators of Delta Force.

Had Haney's work as a Ranger been enough to prepare him for Delta Force? Yes! He was one of only a few who were chosen to train for the first Delta Force unit.

Army Rangers tackle some of the military's toughest missions.

Weapons Training

Haney's Delta Operator Training Course lasted for six months. Each day, **trainees** worked on shooting skills. They practiced firing from different angles. They practiced while standing still and while running. They also practiced shooting alone and as part of a team.

U.S. Army soldiers, like Delta Force operators, train as part of a team.

Soldiers worked with many kinds of **targets**. It was important that they had perfect aim. They knew they would be working to free hostages from enemies.

Delta Force operators work with many types of guns.

U.S. Army soldiers practice shooting at a target.

Hostage Rescue Training

Haney trained in a special house called the Shooting House. Each time trainees raced into the house, objects were set up differently, and targets popped up when least expected. This taught operators how to handle many types of rescues.

Part of the Shooting House looked like the inside of an airplane. **Hijacking** scenes were set up there so trainees could practice rescuing hostages.

These U.S. Army soldiers practice rescuing hostages in a special training house.

Though the official name for the house was the Shooting House, some called it the House of Horrors.

Trainees learned how to move fast and surprise the enemy. They practiced spotting differences between enemies and hostages. They learned how to find people who were lost and take them to safety.

During a training excercise, U.S. soldiers prepare to attack a building.

Special Skills

During training, operators traveled long distances during the day and at night. They worked with powerful explosives. They practiced using ropes to race up and down the sides of buildings. Operators even learned to break into a car, start the engine without a key, and zip around corners at high speeds.

This instructor demonstrates climbing skills during a training session.

Operators were also taught how to leave messages for one another by making chalk marks on buildings and street corners. They would need all these skills when they worked in enemy **territory**.

Trainees also learned to drive right through roadblocks. They practiced ramming other cars to make them stop. These were skills they might need in a rescue.

Delta Force operators also learned to use armed vehicles.

Rescue from Enemy Camp

Since the first Delta Force unit was formed, operators have traveled around the world to rescue Americans. One important rescue happened in the Sudan in 1993. **Guerrillas** had kidnapped a group of Americans. The hostages were being held at an enemy camp in a tiny village.

A village in the Sudan

Delta operators loaded their supplies and special jeeps into a plane. They landed at an **airstrip** near the enemy camp. Along with soldiers from the Sudan, they drove the jeeps out of the plane. As the sun rose, they attacked the camp. The enemy fled. Delta operators found the Americans and whisked them to safety.

The jeeps used by Delta Force operators were equipped with machine guns.

Sudanese soldiers helped Delta Force operators during their mission in the Sudan.

Stopping Enemy Soldiers

Another important Delta mission took place in Mogadishu, Somalia. In 1993, General Mohamed Farrah Aidid declared that all U.S. forces and others working for peace must leave the country. So Delta Force and other military groups were sent over to capture Aidid's soldiers and stop his government.

A U.S. military tank in Mogadishu, Somalia

For this mission, 40 Delta operators flew in 17 helicopters. Operators jumped from the helicopters and made their way inside a nearby house. They captured 22 enemy soldiers.

General Mohamed Farrah Aidid

During the mission in Somalia, some of the helicopters carrying soldiers from other U.S. military groups crashed. Delta operators worked hard to protect soldiers as the enemy arrived and fired on them. Sadly, many American soldiers died.

Capturing Saddam Hussein

In 2003, Delta Force operators traveled to Iraq. The president of the country, Saddam Hussein, had gone into hiding after Iraq was attacked by U.S. troops. Delta Force received word that Saddam Hussein had been found.

Saddam Hussein's hiding spot

Delta Force and other military groups raced to the scene. They forced Hussein out of his hiding place and captured him.

Saddam Hussein had been hiding in a tiny **cellar** at a farmhouse near Tikrit, Iraq.

Working in Secret

Delta Force operators are constantly training. They always need to keep their skills sharp. They never know when they will be called on another important mission.

Green Berets

Today, Delta Force operators may come from any branch of the U.S. armed forces. However, operators often come from the Army Rangers or Green Berets.

Most of Delta Force's work remains a secret. Operators cannot even tell their families what they are doing or where their work will take them. Where will Delta Force missions take the operators in the future? Only time will tell, and the rest of us may never know.

Delta Force Gear

Delta Force operators use different types of airplanes to get to their missions. Here are two of them.

AC-130H Gunship

MC-130 Aircraft

Delta Force operators use many different kinds of weapons while they are on missions. Here are some of them.

M-4 Carbine with M-203 Grenade Launcher

M4-A1 Carbine

MP-5 Machine Gun

Glossary

airstrip (AIR-strip) a flat patch of ground used to land planes

Army Ranger (AR-mee RAYNJ-uhr) a member of the U.S. Army Special Forces who has been specially trained for difficult missions

cellar (SEL-ur) a room below ground level in a house, often used to store things

choppers (CHOP-urz) helicopters

explosives (ek-SPLOH-sivz) substances that can blow up

founding (FOUND-ing) the first to start something

guerrillas (guh-RIL-uhz) members of a group of soldiers fighting against a government or an army

hijacking (HYE-jak-ing) taking illegal control of something, such as an airplane or car, and making the pilot or driver go somewhere

hostage (HOSS-tij) a person held prisoner as a way of demanding money or other things

jumpmaster (JUHMP-mass-tur) the officer in charge of soldiers who are using parachutes to jump out of planes

kidnapped (KID-napt) taken as a prisoner and kept until certain demands are met

missions (MISH-uhnz) special jobs

operators (OP-uh-*ray*-turz) members of Delta Force

parachute jumpers (PA-ruh-shoot JUHMP-urz) people who jump from planes using a soft cloth attached to ropes to help slow down the fall

physical (FIZ-uh-kuhl) having to do with the body

prison (PRIZ-uhn) a place where people are made to live as punishment for committing a crime; jail

targets (TAR-gits) marks or objects that are aimed or shot at

territory (TER-uh-tor-ee) a large area of land

terrorism (TER-ur-iz-im) the act of using violence and threats to achieve goals

trainees (tray-NEEZ) people who are learning to do something by practicing

unit (YOU-nit) a person, thing, or group that is part of a larger group

Bibliography

Beckwith, Charlie A., and Donald Knox. *Delta Force: The Army's Elite Counterterrorist Unit*. San Diego, CA: Harcourt Brace Jovanovich (1983).

Griswold, Terry, and D.M. Giangreco. *Delta: America's Elite Counterterrorist Force*. St. Paul, MN: Zenith Press (2005).

Haney, Eric L. *Inside Delta Force*. New York: Delacorte Press (2003).

www.army.mil/ (official site of the U.S. Army)

Read More

Fridell, Ron. *Spy Technology*. Minneapolis, MN: Lerner (2006).

Richie, Jason. *Iraq and the Fall of Saddam Hussein*. Minneapolis, MN: The Oliver Press (2003).

Zeigler, Heidi. *Bodyguard*. Danbury, CT: Children's Press (2003).

Learn More Online

To learn more about Delta Force, visit
www.bearportpublishing.com/SpecialOps

Index

About the Author

Gail Blasser Riley is the author of more than 400 books, articles, and educational pieces for children and adults. Her books have received honors from the Children's Book Council, New York Public Library, and Young Adult Library Services Association.